W0115064

between
the walls

BOOKS BY PAUL VERMEERSCH

POETRY
Burn (2000)
The Fat Kid (2002)
Between the Walls (2005)

ANTHOLOGY
The I. V. Lounge Reader (2001)

between
the walls

paul vermeersch

M&S

Copyright © 2005 by Paul Vermeersch

All rights reserved. The use of any part of this publication reproduced, transmitted in any form or by any means, electronic, mechanical, photocopying, recording, or otherwise, or stored in a retrieval system, without the prior written consent of the publisher – or, in case of photocopying or other reprographic copying, a licence from the Canadian Copyright Licensing Agency – is an infringement of the copyright law.

Library and Archives Canada Cataloguing in Publication

Vermeersch, Paul
Between the walls / Paul Vermeersch.

Poems.
ISBN 0-7710-8744-6

I. Title.

PS8593.E74B48 2004   C811'.6   C2004-905955-6

We acknowledge the financial support of the Government of Canada through the Book Publishing Industry Development Program and that of the Government of Ontario through the Ontario Media Development Corporation's Ontario Book Initiative. We further acknowledge the support of the Canada Council for the Arts and the Ontario Arts Council for our publishing program.

Text design by Sean Tai
Typeset in Bembo by M&S, Toronto
Printed and bound in Canada

This book is printed on acid-free paper that is 100% recycled, ancient-forest friendly (100% post-consumer recycled).

McClelland & Stewart Ltd.
The Canadian Publishers
481 University Avenue
Toronto, Ontario
M5G 2E9
www.mcclelland.com

1 2 3 4 5   09 08 07 06 05

This book is dedicated to Chris Banks.

Contents

II AS FIELDS BECOME BIRDS BECOME CLOUDS

III   AS IS

I

Garbage Day

THE LIGHTS KEEP CHANGING

The lights keep changing. Cars and trucks
are nudged into motion by the winking
permission of a green signal, and a grey pigeon

undistinguished from the million others
roosting quietly in the city's details
is startled by the sudden noise of traffic.

Launched now into mindless flight by a silent
alarm in its seedcase brain, the frightened bird
hops and jumps and is clipped by a passing Audi.

A wing hangs broken and motionless.
A wing flaps flaps flaps in its panic.
One eye sees nothing while the other stares

at chrome wheels turning in clouds of exhaust,
feathers and guttertrash stirred and tossed
in the wake of a streetcar charging west.

Unique among his dull grey neighbours now
the injured pigeon staggers in the street
confused in its movements, as though searching

for a reason, anything to help it make sense
of the pain, but there is no reason — only
a moving van speeding through the amber

for the *coup de grâce*, and there is no grieving,
no chorus of mournful coos from the millions
that remain, and nothing comes to a halt

but one grey bird, and the lights keep changing.

GIRL ON A BALCONY

From her balcony, she sees the whole thing broiling:
rough neighbourhood where the fed-up go-girl honey
boots the wolf-whistle B-boy in the nuts,

the brawls behind curtains and deals going down,
down by the schoolyard where a brief blip of siren
sends jumpy sneakers scuttling over the chain-link.

The streets dictate every kind of filthy upheaval:
late-night trash-talking bastards revving old vendettas,
acres of toddlers stuffed in plastic chairs in shitty diapers,

bad-blood tainted sofa sex while the water runs,
a smoke burns down in the ashtray, and a girl
learns exactly what she can never tell her mother.

When it's over she stands on the balcony
and blows a kiss to all the cold blue lips
in all the quiet bathtubs in the world,

blows the same smoke rings she's been blowing
since she turned thirteen, as the neighbourhood sings
the song of wet fingers stroking the crystal rim.

All around the black flies spark in the rusty zappers,
and the big ones crackle for a long, long time.
She hovers in the ultraviolet light, being eaten.

URBAN VIOLENCE WITH STARLINGS

Birds are grasped in the palm,
little wicker hand grenades
with feathers to muffle the blast –

and boys, in love with their failures,
conceal their shuttlecocks, carry
their starlings into schools and restaurants

teeming with barriers – they collide,
bumping shoulders, they rut
over money, symbolic castrations, a girl –

that's how it starts – a starling flaps
inside a coat pocket,
a heart beating out of control

outside of its body, and later
an ambulance wails to the scene
through a blizzard of black down.

THE RISE AND FALL OF THE CATS IN HIS GRANDPARENTS' BARN

All will live and die inside
two hundred yards of their birth-site,
as term after gruelling term
the females produce six to ten
pink hors d'oeuvres apiece,
six-fingered, nipple-gnawing kittens
picking banjos of mouse-gut.

An old tomcat, their Adam,
relaxes in the rafters on the nights
the sky runs clear. He watches
the dawns arrive in increments,
radiant beams of dust that burst
through ratty gaps in the clapboard,
slicing their shadows to bits.

From his perch he spies his sister,
their Eve, looking ancient,
ragged and matronly, the well-spring
of all these congenital snags, these
taboo offspring of taboo offspring.
Now a new litter grows in her belly
while another is still on the teat.

This class is governed by tooth and nail
and sired by thorn-bearing penis.
Their chieftains have seen Goliaths
sink unwelcome litters whole,
in rain barrels, in rivers,

flimsy and blind, but cat enough yet
to mewl to their ill-bred gods.

The extra toes repeat themselves
until at last they don't seem strange.
One generation is born deaf, the next
encephalitic, deranged, dog-eaten, dunked,
and done. They have no tales of origin,
their descendants will have no myths
of how it was once . . . or how it got like this.

THE DAISY. THE DOLPHIN. THE DAGGER. THE DRAGON.

She bites her lip, her secret, and reclines in the chair,
thoughtful of permanence, of pain, and the floral
skin of an ancestor's father that hangs
in a modern museum, stretched and tanned:

a red-faced monkey shows its fangs, a warrior
advances through a forest of swords, and there
a wave bearing a golden ship crashes hard against
black rocks strewn across the ancient man's flanks.

The needle hums with childlike electricity, depositing
the hammer and chisel and the old ochre dye.
In her modesty she orders the cobalt dragon placed
against the semicircle of her hipbone, out of sight.

She's quietly closed the door on all her weaknesses.
Now part of her will always be strong and fierce.
The blue-scaled body in smoke and flame is the sign
of the needle that marks her in muscle and mind.

GIRL ON A TALK SHOW (HER AMPHIBIAN)

Monday morning accompanies the vomit kiss, the amphibian
grows in the belly; the ring constricts the ring finger
as the finger grows thick and the lungfish plumps
into legfish, into mammal, growing larger in the amniotic
    bath.

It began with a kiss, the amphibian, in a flask, in a rush
of hemoglobin mixed with whisky-soured spit, it began
without the usual precautions, and until the decision was
    made
to let it live, she could not think of it except as amphibian.

Evolution replays itself in miniature, from blastula to brain
until, at last, the thing is born – pink, human, whole –
and even then she fears she cannot love or that she'll shudder
at the thought of her own child's new tongue flicking at her
    milk.

She fears the mirrorballs, like Earth, have ceased their spinning,
that her champagne has thickened to pabulum; she does not
    want
the collapse of her youth that slept in her womb to wake
coughing in a nursery filled with flowers and bears.

TAKE 1 TABLET(S) DAILY

Twenty mils paroxetine HCl. Two weeks in mania;
    this is the free ride, bad case
of the giggles on doctors' samples, kite-high.

When you settle in there's a calm, there's
    an *ahh* that skims over
the silver ocean in a hoverchair, breezy and noiseless,

but then you notice: legs are electric, technorealism
    in dreamvision, alien feelings
that come in peace, bug-eyed, and strange things below.

Not sure when the lethargy thickens, but it's ingrown
    like a second skeleton
without joints. Contentment becomes apathy, marble,

and the statue on the hill can't feel the wind,
    all made of stone.

THE IRON GATES

God save the Queen, the iron gates
of Buckingham are everywhere.
They span the ocean and snake
through our streets, keeping things,
people, buildings, in their place.
From a courtyard's distance,
just there, we see tall princes,
we can't imagine who they are
but we know they are princes
on their way somewhere, walking,
dressed in suits, in light blue sweaters,
but again, we can't imagine where.

Outside the gates what causes ache
at dinner tables, the meanness
of the feast, the meagre
meals dished out with love
or resentment or resignation,
stale bread reheated in a shell
of moistened foil, a resurrection
of the spoils of last week's pay,
what was earned with sweat and breath
and toil, or worse, long hours
of boredom on tired feet, just enough
to fake it through another day,
at least until the next cheque clears,
and then with luck there might be more.

And then there might be seedless grapes
in china bowls, pale green gems

that rot if not enjoyed. There might be grapes
or pears or fresh-cut beef, depending
on what's left when debts are lessened
and the rent is paid and the Queen
takes her share behind the iron gates,
her share of beef, of pears, of grapes,
and new blue sweaters for her sons.

PORCELAIN HORSES

Sometimes, when you are looking at a horse
made of delicate blue-veined porcelain
and maybe this horse is a hundred
or even a thousand years old

you feel a little pang of disappointment
because it wasn't smashed to pieces
when it should have been; it goes on
defying mortality, dragging

its maker's name through the centuries
a small red circular pictograph
meaning Earth and Fire
like a captive bound at the wrists.

And you imagine sunburned archaeologists
joyfully unearthing it from blackened soil
alongside remnants of weapons
and broken armour, where great warriors

once fought and spilled blood in order
to possess this horse, to bring it home
and place it on the hearth, because
even they required something precious

to remind them why they even bother
getting up in the mornings, day after day
putting on their Dark Age suits and ties
and heading off to the office of battle.

This morning I racked my brain trying
to remember what gets me out of bed.
Today my porcelain horse was an appointment
with my doctor. I sat in the waiting room

reading an article on Chinese ceramics
while a man prepared to warn me about
smoking, drinking, and an unhealthy diet.
We choose our own battles. Life today

is still as ruthless as ever. I know this
from eavesdropping on a conversation
down the hall – the warriors might be gone
but it's someone else's Dark Age now.

Another blastoma has been discovered
in the retina maybe, or in the lung
of someone's daughter, and tomorrow
another battle will begin.

Maybe they should give her a porcelain horse
to ride into this tiny war. Perhaps
she won't be disappointed with its flawless
blue glaze, its ability to last

a thousand years. And maybe they should
tell her about the warriors, how they fought
to possess something precious, explain to her
that only the one who fights bravest

can keep that horse and call it her own.
Maybe they should ask her to name it
and imagine herself sitting safely on its back,
protected from the marauding horde of cells —

before the two of them, both so fragile, slip
and shatter into a million little pieces.

EARTHQUAKE AND FRAGMENT

Gradually the disease stole
the knife and fork from her hands,
the laces from her boots, a pair
for pastures and a pair for church,
identical. It took her upper plate,
her letter L, her husband's name
and the gravity from her prayers
                    and admonitions.

Creeping through cells through
mild sins and sharp synapses
it came and went and took
her afternoon walk sometimes–
with sometimes–without her,
leaving her in the living room
living misinformed, filching
her daily paper from the stoop
replacing the cheaply printed words
                    with balderdash.

Little by little it spread
from her body to her chair
from her chair to the house
shaking when she shook, rattling
her lights, the hundred-year-old
china in the hutch, drumming
its music on the various bottles
of pills in the pantry that spill
here and there to the floor.
Everything was earthquake and fragment

and alive in the vanishing pulse
                of her body.

The disease then in its mindlessness
made a nest in her sleep, swaddling
her spine in heavy chains, restraining
her grasp, her gait, her gaze,
and gradually, like her, the disease
turned white and none could find her
through the raging snow of her disease,
until she was lost and she was always
getting lost . . . even in the mail,
                her ashes.

LAWN KINGS

They hate one another in triumph, in the thick green carpets
of their neighbours, and lovingly, jokingly,
they hate one another in defeat, in the dry brown patches,
in the white explosive crowns of dandelions,

and still they stand united to shake their fists against weather
and policy.

Collecting cans at grocery stores, they rally round
the one whose daughter fell to meningitis,
and together in their unused nights, as if by prior treaty,
by tacit neighbourly accord, they do not touch their wives,

but still they are divided on the subjects of dogshit and
leaves.

And though they hate one another on Sundays, they gather
in a great white hall under man-made light and
lovingly, jokingly, they listen to an argument for decency
without which they fear they would all turn to sin.

BRIGHTS GROVE

Old Waterworks Road still divides
     the original village into richer
and poorer. That side: all creaking,
     windy cottages where long ago
tourists flocked to spend their idle
     lakeside summers. And this:
where some are building taller
     lakefront homes of fired brick.
And farther down Lake Huron's shore
     a half-forgotten bandshell sloughs
off a cracking skin of jaundiced
     lemon-yellow paint and crumbles
into yesteryear, where rails once stopped
     to unload leisure-class travellers
in search of picnic land and the tuneful
     pleasures of Dixieland, waltzes
and hot swing through the night.

Its former joys are toppled now
in disarray. In Wildwood Park
        a pair of vestigial lakeside cabins,
painted red, once marked
        the site of quiet getaways
from the headaches of business –
        the Labatt family's hideout
from the inland stink of yeast
        in developing London. They're
nothing now but tumbledown
        shacks, chained and padlocked,
boarded up. But Brights Grove's
        straydog youth, grown coarse
in their boredom, break through
        those planks and huddle to escape
through their hash pipes and crack
        pipes into reckless covert orgies
on the floors of broken glass.
        This new revelry, where roaches
thicken, is what charms them
        and hardens their skin to a town
with no industry but the next town's
        dying chemical valley, where
the too-green grass and the floating
        fish are equally unnatural.

On the borders where the odours
        of Saran Wrap and pigshit commingle,
Brights Grove's commuters work
        temp jobs, in positions that meant
pensions to their fathers, scrubbing
        oil refinery tanks dressed up
like giant baseballs, happy faces,
        or placid purple spheres on which
the word of god is painted,
        a message to this new breed
of low-paid employees: "Be thou
        content with such things as ye have,"
like polypropylene and creosote —
        the products of their labour that
have built this region where no bird
        or leaf lasts one season unassailed
by leakage above the legal
        parts per million, where weekend-
sailors and farming people wonder
        if the old Dow Blob still crawls
the Saint Clair's bottom,
        or if the latest spill has leached
into the township's drinking water,
        though most would rather turn
their thoughts to golf balls
        and backyard chores, forget the rot
that's settled in and pay the bills.

Driving home's the best part
of the day, not getting there,
    but driving, when you could
still be headed anywhere.
    But home is home. It's where
your bones repair, where the stories
    of your life are told and where
your own bright star can rise
    and maybe shine until some
future spring, when the water
    might finally be clean again,
and the old music will play
    in the bandshell by the lake again,
and the well-dressed travellers
    and the kissing young will return
like migratory birds to the shore.

But if that doesn't happen,
if your bones still ache
        and your stories aren't told,
and the tourists and the lovers
        keep their money and their distance
from the place you've always lived,
        and if the bandshell is little more
than a great deaf ear washed up
        on a polluted beach, then maybe
it will still be good enough
        to know you've made it home.
You can stop the car, go inside,
        and rest until tomorrow.

THE ARMIES OF PLUTO

They're impossible to count,
the forgotten ones marching
across the mind's distant horizon,
disappearing like old phone numbers
or minor injuries, all the people
I've met but can't remember meeting
except for scraps of faces
when I rub my eyes years later,
the many thousand nameless ones
who've touched my life
so faintly they left no mark.

Sometimes the faces linger,
phosphorescent bodies glow
in geologic eras of beerfog,
evening upon evening of hands
shaken across wobbly tables,
but what have I done
with their names? I have made them
legion and sent them down
to clash with the armies of Pluto.

When I was seven or eight, I sat
on my father's knee surrounded
by elderly men who spoke
no English that I could understand.
I remember a kitchen done up
in yellow curtains and a broad
wooden table from another time.
I remember a glass of pink juice,

a plate of warm raisin cookies
and the smell of fresh coffee.

But I do not remember
the elderly men. I see them
only through a haze, stiff
and lifeless, like totem poles
to scare me in the forest
and mark the place of my forgetfulness.
I can remember they smelled
of liverwurst and bleated
like goats in a sudden downpour
whenever a joke was told.
Their raucous old-world laughter
still hasn't left me, but what
have I done with their names?
I have sent them deep under
into battle with the others.

GARBAGE DAY

You, jarred from sleep half an hour
before the alarm by an idling engine and
the hydraulic crush of busted kitchen chairs
from down the block. It doesn't help

that you've been having trouble sleeping lately,
and what was it you forgot to do last night?
Sorting sleep from life, it all comes back –
the shattered oven door, the ruined rug.

Barefoot in pyjamas behind the garage you find
cans upended and bags torn open, damn dog,
and the godforsaken shovel's broken. It doesn't help
that you've been worried about your job

since the latest round of renegotiations.
Everything you've pitched the last seven days
is lying scattered at your feet. So many things
have gone to waste . . . you never knew.

A laden can in each hand, biceps working
with back pain, bare feet on gravel, ruts
and puddles. It's almost too much. The truck
is already at your neighbour's house.

One more can to fetch. Forget it. Let it be.
The first cars of morning have already started.
Your neighbours are rolling slowly past your driveway
and you know they know they've beaten you.

TALL MAN WITH DOG AND RABBITS
for Chris

Small wild rabbits live
      in constant fright behind
           your lettuce patch.
Cardiac explosives
      on hair-trigger switches.
           Zip toys. Foreign hats.

I've seen you gingerly
      mow around their nest,
           the jujube kits in neat piles,
leaving behind a knee-high ring
      of dying grass by summer's end.
           And with the chores done
you rest, almost alone
      in the hammock of Saturday
           with breeze in your crabapple tree
and your dog half-asleep
      keeping your relaxed breath
           within careful earshot,
his chest filled with marrow,
      your chest filled with a private
           kind of rock and roll.

And the rabbits, alive
      in their blind nest, hear it too —
           through the same ridiculous ears
that know the rain is falling
      before it hits the earth.
           To them you are weather

and landslide, friend,
     moving above them
          like distant thunder
or a mountain about to fall.
     Quiet now. Listen.
          Breathing now.
Everything breathes with you.
     How long has it been
          since you weren't this tall?

BECOMING BEAUTIFUL

This year the cicada has returned to be the hideous pest
    crawling in the trees
        instead of me. I have come
  down from the willow, down
from the tangle of grieving boughs, in order to be beautiful.

No more will I shriek in the treetops, in search of a suitable
    mate.
    The cicada does that well enough
        and I have new-found ambitions:
    to become beautiful, rare
as a white gorilla, like the one that died of cancer
                in Barcelona.

Have a drink and we'll toast to my improvements:
    my four fabulous limbs,
        my dolphin-smooth skin.
    And here, where my claws once
ended in warts, my hands will soon be those of a boy
             in a painting.

I will have Samson's hair, the waistline of a greyhound.
    My eyes will mirror
        the late-rising April sun.
    And when I'm through becoming beautiful,
the red-eyed choir will sing my arrival, in the trees,
             for two weeks.

II

As Fields Become Birds Become Clouds

AS FIELDS BECOME BIRDS BECOME CLOUDS

Drawing Snoopy on the mirror after bath time, this naked
little boy in the steam, printing a thumb for the nose,

then another, standing on the vanity, another
white muzzle, another black nose, and the mirror,

as fields become birds become clouds, an Escher of Snoopies.

There is a love at work here, and a solar system, and epochs
crashing through time as floors through a levelled building.

He is clean now, and the rest should be painless.
The steam will evaporate, and the love, and the boy.

THE DIFFICULTY OF FORGIVING SUMMER

How could he find it in his heart
to absolve the algal bloom
that closed summer's last enjoyable beach
as the sweltering August heat
was reaching its zenith?
On the hottest days, the stench
of baby painted turtles trapped and drowned
in backyard swimming pool leaf skimmers
rose above the smell of roasting corn.

At night there were swarms
        of insects with no mouths.

An old neighbour, he recalls,
wore that heat on her brow
in drops that ran like quicksilver
down her face and soaked into her hair
as the thermometer's mercury rose,
and it was clear she was being consumed
by something inhuman.

During one such unbearably warm vacation
finally at his zenith, he stopped growing any taller,
but as he listened carefully at night
he could still hear the corn,
kilometres away, stretching out of the soil
toward the permanent stars, until
only the corn could see over the corn,
and it was levelled by machines.

The afternoons were filled with chainsaws
felling birch and backhoes hollowing
the earth, dotting summer's face with
towering hills of soil that stood for years,
home to a million stinging weeds.

At night a horror of mayflies
        descended on everything.

FEEDING THE DEER

Marineland 1987

What I was before and then after
I was bitten by the glorious white-tailed buck
were as far removed as velvet and bone.

Deer don't bite. I was that naive.
I dropped my cone of dog food to the pavement.
A claret bruise blossomed in my soft underarm.

None of us knows why we are free
or not free. Nothing with so many thorns
in its belly could ever be fed by hand.

Velvet peeled away from my heart,
my delicate pericardium, shocked
that something beautiful did not love me.

I grew six terrible inches.
My bones hardened
into their permanence.

NOTES TOWARD A LEXICON OF THE LANGUAGE OF THE BEAR

I

In its own language its name means:

I walk slowly on hillsides
and sleep with a bellyful
of pleasing berries,
pink flesh, and brains.

I dream of love vulgar
and gorgeous beside the rush
of rivers born of glacial ice
and I shun the times
of no plenty, when all is dark
and white and the blossoms
do not love the red fruit into being.

This is the simplest word in its language
and the first one it learns.

II

The bear does not have a word for regret
but the nearest equivalent would be:

> *I am not proud*
> *to have gone to the end of the world*
> *and eaten garbage there*
> *in dumps among the naked and the thin*
> *when I could not last the winter.*

This word is often thought but seldom
spoken among the strong.

III

If you want to say I love you
in the bearish tongue say:

> *You need not fear me*

and translated literally
the word for solitude is:

> *This side of the mountain is mine.*

STRANGLED

From the waist down a woman, but the rest
    all mermaid, the crashing wash
of sea spray in her voice. That slender neck,
    the swan-envied pivot
of her neck, cousin to a length of ivory tusk,
    but soft, the white belly
of a diving bird gone wild on the dark
    ferocious surface of the sea, the box
in which she hides her lethal dart,
    the tremendous pianoforte of her song.

She sang a shy, unwilling listener to the rocks,
    a song so sleepless and cloudy and strangled
that her visitor quietly wept
    from his invisible third eye.

—

A SUDDEN PLAGUE OF TOADS

The car is skidding, sliding
in a fog both airborne and mental
as sabre-toothed butterflies
rise in the driver's belly
and his mind closes like a toad's
eyelid, blind to the fright
of it all, the unthinkable truth,
these dark streets paved
with a sudden plague of toads.
They leap by the thousands
from rain-flooded ditches
that border the nearby fields.
Thousands, tens of thousands,
they appear on the road
without thought or warning
like spiteful words blurted
in a spat between lovers.

Last year, ten years ago, twenty,
it was snakes. Clusters of them
writhed in window wells
and choked on newborn toads
in the lilac park. Back then
the roads were paved with
snakes' black skins, and boys
brought pails of them home,
living things for purposes
both innocent and sinister,
and there were snakes threshed
like stalks in the wheat fields
or carried out of local schools
in plastic grocery bags.

And now his car is skidding,
sliding, and his mind
winks suddenly open —
the butterflies settle
in their pit as he takes
his hand away from hers
to wrestle with the wheel,
regaining control of the car,
of his life, both their lives,
and his thoughts race
through a mental checklist:
which way to turn, how hard
to step on the accelerator.

But it's happening too fast.
He must struggle to be sure.
This may be the last time
he feels this way about dying,
about a future as unruly
as the present, about the girl
who's sitting next to him
and the many promises
they've made to each other.
The fog is beginning to lift.
The gas station up ahead
looks clean and lit, looks safe.

SACRAMENTS

You never made me holy, never
confessed, never told me
exactly what went down in Montreal,
what made the ivory birds of June
shrink hysterically from our approach.

Instead . . . instead you baptized me,
plunged my head into the icy stream,
pressing it under longer than you needed
to bestow on me the lowly name
of the foul-mouthed pagan's donkey.

In the long-eared wandering that followed,
I discovered new sacraments:
of addiction and emaciation,
the transcendent sacrament of medication,
and the sublime rite of drunken regret.

Though, priestess, now I'm an apostate
and my devotion is behind me,
I still sometimes habitually
turn my pink face to Montreal,
and in my brick-and-mortar room

I contemplate the mysteries.

CHERRY BLOSSOMS IN AN ORCHARD

Someone remembers smoke rising from holes
drilled in teeth, the search for dull metal
in the back of the mouth, the glint
of an earring lost in the elbow of a drain.

Someone remembers a bicycle crushed
by a car, an antelope crushed by a car,
and a chicken's egg tossed in a picnic game
landing safely in a plastic cup.

Someone remembers cherry blossoms in an orchard.
Scandalous white blossoms, his favourite little
　　　　　　　　　　　what's-her-names.

And he remembers them not because of their scent
or because August fattened their green gushing
ovaries into hard sour fruit, but because a dry summer
brought mice, and the mice attracted owls.

And there was gluttony among the mice and delight
among the owls, such that at picking time
the trees were bare and the soles of his boots
snapped on grass packed with tiny grey bones.

And what's-her-name, that flower, was shaking
in the doorway, blaming him. And he hasn't been
　　　　　　　　　　　home in twelve years.

EVEN BEATEN HORSES HAVE GHOSTS

Beaten to death months ago, the broken horse,
the grudge borne against defeat
born of her colourless eyes, her twisted back,
and his tearful confession
on that first half-decent day in spring.

That confession foaled an ignorant colt
between them, wild and ugly.
And though it was clearly no thoroughbred,
he called it Valentine. She called it valueless,
and whipped it with apologies at first
and later venom. She knocked that horse
until it couldn't stand, but through it all
he swore it was a champion. This swayback nag,
she whooped, this tube of glue! Her laughter
entered from a distance, like bullets.

And even now, should she arrive,
he'll smile politely, count to ten,
though cursed by the visions:
her pumpkin head, his pumpkin heart,
the fiery hooves crashing through the fields.

BEASTS

Going with you as far as the corner that night,
I might have been naked in the city's equatorial heat,

but with all that humidity, the broad air touching me,
I wouldn't have noticed. I might have been naked.

My muscles were alive on my bones like beasts in trees.
They howled through the night for your nearness;

they moved, higher and higher, into their kingdom.
Darling, they thought the rains had come.

THE WAY SOME THINGS ARE ALMOST TOO GREY

Industrial dove gunmetal smoke
battleship slate: you need them all
to copy a sky like this.
It's autumn almost, or already.

The earliest cramps of SAD
contract and expand in the grey matter
and a grey memory abruptly snaps
into colour on that sky.

Today is not the worst day
in a man's life. He is steady
and sober after a good breakfast.
His clothes are clean and warm

and he has recently known the touch
of tender hands on the small of his back.
But in the memory, he is broken
and inconsolable. In the memory,

she is speaking, her voice a sonic boom
approaching from across an infinite plain,
heading for a small grey shell
where all will gather itself, in time.

There are pieces torn away
from old desires, old needs,
glass and nails, faith and vows. They rattle
in the shell as the storm draws near.

There is a small grey corner of plastic
broken off a favourite toy,
and the sky is as grey as his reasons
for not going with her to St. John's.

BETWEEN THE WALLS

That there's lightning is a guess he's only too willing
to hazard; thunder shakes the windows
almost as often as raindrops moisten them, but exterior light
doesn't come here, not even in slivers. The centipedes

won't hear of it. A plate of eggs will have to do
and some toast of course and one of the fuzzy channels
the TV's been receiving lately. He has it pretty good, he'd say,
though the work hasn't been enough. There are three

pills left, but he's been in the pink recently and figures
he'll just quit taking them, skip the refill and cling
to the hope that things will pick up with work, say,
and the doctor, and the rain will stop eventually,

and the centipedes, instead of drying out between the walls,
will softly fade away or turn into silvery flakes of money.

PREPARATIONS FOR THE WINNING TICKET

Willing to wait, he didn't need to know
how many hours would pass, or days.
The occasion would be monstrous, a gala,
as the homecoming of the once-and-future
or the return of the only begotten. Big,
such that he was willing to hold off on minor
luxuries like salted butter, like cigarettes
or any entertainment of the flesh, so as to devote
himself entirely to the vital preparations.

He long ago resolved to live in endless Lent
so his sacrifices would roll a red carpet
through the desert, a carpet his meticulous
details would weave: hospital corners
drawn tight, napkins in their napkin rings, ashes
in their urns, the linoleum waxed to a shine.

HOLDING THE INFANT CHIMPANZEE ORPHANED BY POACHERS IN GABON FELT SURPRISINGLY SELF-REFERENTIAL

Something in his brown eyes, no more
or less brown than the eyes of my uncle,
knew he was more likely than the others
to smoke cigarettes and wear red shorts

someday, and something else, a deeper,
more substantial knowledge that he was
alone in the universe, that all the green leaves
on Earth wouldn't make him more human,

that he should never have to try, that being
a clown was enough, and when not a clown,
the silent master of a single thought, and this
should suffice, this, and knowing death

is somehow absolute, there is no turning
back from it, no moving forward either.

LITTLE RED FLAGS

Leaving his cash and plastic on the cluttered
kitchen table, he took a yellow page torn
from the phone book, indexed Golf
to Gun Shops, and drove his old beater downtown.

November frost clinging to his sleeves,
he choked on the cold and checked out
the models – hazy, he couldn't tell you
the names of the irons he handled.

To him they were: *tin can, neighbour,
goddamn squirrel*, and *gag reflex*, in that order,
and reaching for his wallet he remembered
his promise: *No buying today, just browsing.*

Wanting only to hold them, to see how it felt
to be a different kind of man, if only briefly,
then cruise around town in no great hurry,
relax in the park and watch the pigeons peck

survival from the ice, watch the dogs chase
rubber balls through snow as bundled children
run and tumble, turn blue, fight, and wipe
their noses on their mittens till they all go blurry.

Little red flags were popping up all over the place.
He started seeing holes in everything.

THE MISSION HOUSE

From that day forth his life was aftermath.
The streets were grubby, his fever hot,
the water in his glass was aftermath,
and he laid his blame evenly like snow.

He mourned a happy job on King Street
as he might have mourned the fall of Rome.
He felt old friendships like noiseless deer
receding into various alpine landscapes.

One he called brother fell silent and then
went into the snows and never returned.
Forests of crimson and gold were levelled to ash
beyond the borders his heart's forbearance.

He weighed Cain's rock against Delilah's shears.
He saw the shallow grave and the temple in ruins.
There was a great swell of voices followed by silence.
Even as he fled from it, he sensed that unseen hands
        were preparing his cot in the mission house.

SORRY I'M LATE

You wait for me, looking now and then at your watch,
where small gold hands sweep the white lunar face
of your ideal patience. I know you've been waiting
to tell me your theory about the rain:

the rain of ancient scrolls, the river breaching its levy,
the flood plains overwhelmed and the flock drowned –
their defenceless bodies found in the washed-out gully
when the radio signals all clear.
                              Sorry I'm late.
I've been anxious to hear you talk about the rain.
Now the water is rising and you're soaked to the skin.
If I lived near the river, I'd have thought of the river.
If I only knew your name, I would be there by now.

BUT I WAS LOOKING AT THE PERMANENT STARS
after Wilfred Owen

Not at the planes passing overhead,
their passengers speeding toward
reunions and funerals, snapshots
and forgiveness. Not at the heart-stricken
preparing themselves on ledges.

And not at the highbeams as they approach
from the oncoming lane, watching
in the mirror as they collapse
into the smouldering eyes of hindsight.

Pulling his car onto the shoulder
of a dark road, he fell across the gravel
and screamed into the corn. Where he knelt
there was a depression in the grass
where something had been, a child's
plastic wading pool or the hood of a car.

And the moon was in a regrettable state
of slimness. Someone, he muttered,
someone's got to take the moon
into a corner and teach it the new rules.

He was no longer interested in transience,
in what's been lost. He knew his prognosis.
But I was looking at the permanent stars, he said.

HE WILL NOT DROWN HIS SORROWS

Man to man.

If only I knew more about the human heart,
I could fuel its fire or stamp it out
completely. If only I knew more
about songbirds, I could tell you
exactly what is singing there unseen
in that tree across the street – that song
has been, so far, the best part of my day,
a song as old as our four-chambered hearts,
older maybe, a melody composed a million
years ago and never altered – surely
musical genius thrived before the wheel,
before our weapons and our calculus,
and when we're gone that song
will continue in the trees and will not change.

But we know that song, too. We were born
with its notes and rests transcribed
in the cells of our own warm blood
and we've sung it more or less
unsuccessfully in a hundred-odd cities
between us, lone birds in full throat,
joyous and unheard. And we've fallen
silent, sullen, drunk, when our song
has failed too often. But not that bird
across the street – he will not drown
his sorrows, because he has none.
He will sing until his lady comes or,
in her place, his death, always proud, always

singing, and you know as well as I do
what he does not feel: the bitterness
of solitude, and you also understand
there are times when, if I could catch him,
I would break his neck and end it
so he will not have to sing his song alone.

LAMBS

Kneeling at the fence and reaching through,
you lay your hands upon the lambs.

Never this close before, their sinlessness
is in you now, flowing like a current

from fingertip to fingertip, radiating
from deep beneath the virgin fleece,

and your life feels suddenly criminal,
suddenly wolfish, somehow, clothed in their wool.

Nothing that you've lived through
has prepared you to believe in harmlessness,

that any gaze could be this devoid of purpose,
that such surrender, such lack of want

was ever possible, and now, faced with the lambs,
you begin to sob as though helpless,

the faint lines of turquoise, the veins at your temples,
flooding quietly with their blood.

III

As Is

I

AS IT IS WITH THE BEAUTY OF RIVERS

Be happy about the confetti-
coloured ripples pinwheeling

over the surface of the slow-
moving water. Be happy

the river's flushed cheek
is pretty enough in the sun

we can forget what lies in its belly:
the corroding, half-digested wrecks

that divers never found, old cars
swallowed whole, cinder blocks,

shopping carts, an unsolved
puzzle of bones in the mud,

ribs and tibias, femurs and teeth –
the roiling current struggles

to hold them down. Be happy
the beauty of rivers has this decency.

Because all rivers wish to be Lethe
they flow ever downhill toward it

only to join it where they pass
into brackish grottos, and still

this thing or that comes bubbling
up to the light, something suddenly

remembered, either on the stand
or prodding at the conscience

that rests in the dark. The gentle
nagging we pretend we didn't hear,

the driftwood we sail past pretending
it's driftwood, the joke we tell:

the river, denial, denial. And still,
though the ankles have been fastened

with wire, what the river washes
into the sprawling delta, what rises

to the surface in the Bay of Our Wrongs
is the absolute corpse of As Is.

II

AS IT IS WITH THE LIFE–GIVING SUN

A dog left in the sun will whine
its last idea of baffled love

before it dies, a slow leak
of last breath, as the radio

echoes the nonsense of its life
in the seat of a sweltering Buick.

For the dog of an AM listener
the end is a soft-spoken fact.

For the dog of an FM listener
the end has a false enthusiasm.

A husband and father is humbled
before the courts because

his dog did not perish in that hot car.
It was his daughter instead.

The radio speaks of places where traffic
crawls to a frustrated halt,

of the stomach's pit that deepens
and the medicine that fills it.

It tells a story of rivers breaching
their sandy, shifting banks

in a state with rain. The radio
speaks of centigrade and song.

III

AS IT IS (FOR SOME) IN METROPOLIS

We climb the sunrise steps in hup–
two-three-four fashion, ascending

shafts of fluorescent light in aluminum
crates to the top of the zig-

zag tower, or we drop
in shadow, in droves, in uniform

below the city, below the clock and robot.
Wherever it is we go – we go to work.

We work in offices, on floors
of blood, indignantly, in vapour

rising from our toil, in pursuit
of stunted monthly recompense

to pay for food that coats
our hearts in lethal grease.

And we withdraw, left–
right-left, at the whistle,

returning to see daylight exhausting
its surplus, and marvel in the alleys

at speculation's actual catastrophes,
rummaging for table scraps

in the wash of barely eking.
And it is then, when we are spent,

we might look up in the sky,
hopeful for some sign of mercy

but in the blue above Metropolis
there is no bird, or plane, or anyone.

IV

AS IT IS WITH SLOW-MOVING TRAFFIC

As it is, heading home, some lives
are no longer there at all.

An absent life makes a sound
like a singular peacock calling out

across a great expanse of broadcast towers
and withered birches, trees

that rise like bent and petrified
columns of smoke into the crime-scene

afternoon air, and while everything
that calls out craves an answer

too often the only rejoinders
are the strains of distant traffic.

Slowly in our cars we creep
home, with our minds on chicken

and laundry, home, through the city's
crumbling arteries, listening

to the radio that tells us it's happened
again and the manhunt has begun,

tells us where the hand was found
but not what it was holding, and we

don't have to imagine such trinkets
as plastic barrettes or skipping stones,

the charms of temporary joy.
We know they exist.

V

AS IT IS WITH CHARITY

There is a lost city of people
you don't see begging for change

any more. They used to be there
every day, same clothes, same corners.

Some say they've gone to an island.
There are clues in ancient texts

about such events, about the meek,
the poor-in-spirit; there's always

something about a leper, or a blind man
soliciting alms from the rich,

but inevitably, as the stories go,
some nymph or leprechaun arrives

in the nick of time with a map
to a city of gold, a glorious palace

furnished with the bits and bobs
the rest of us don't want: our old couch

left for trash but rescued
by the itinerant elves of recycling,

garbage bags stuffed to splitting
with the clothes we wore before the kids,

all kindly donated to the needy
citizens of Xanadu or Shangri-La,

of Atlantis or Brigadoon,
or the Union Street YMCA.

VI

AS IT IS WITHOUT

A small hole, smaller
than a chigger's grave,

like the cavity behind
an incisor, the starting point

to a hobo's string of pearls,
or the setting for a missing silver star.

There is a little hollow
where we store our wants,

our feast of everything untasted.
It sometimes feels as vast as Africa.

A man the locals call The General
marches through the neighbourhood,

past the park where he nearly
froze to death in April

sleeping in a ravine, exposed
and drunk when the last snows came.

The General marches. He gathers
an army of plastic bags, carving

a niche for himself, a grave,
a small hole. Smaller.

VII

AS IT IS IN PRIMETIME

Life ends with fierce regularity
on Wednesdays. The detectives

find her come to an end
between bulwarks of wet brick,

deserted among dumpsters and cans,
smart clothes torn to shreds,

skull crushed with a crowbar,
all arranged for private viewing

in a bombardment of cathode rays
directly beamed into our eyes.

A pathologist works late with swabs,
fragments of bone and black light.

He determines time-of-death
by the growth of larvae in her skin.

He tells us she'd been shopping
for wine or meeting a friend

or getting some evening air,
but now she's paperwork,

a routine investigation, the evidence
he's gathered means paperwork,

court appearances, testimony,
cross-examinations, paperwork.

But the voyeurs gather to the edges
of their seats, rapt by the mystery,

the details of morgue-life,
or maybe bolstered in their sense

of civic pride by the cold
communal outrage of the news.

It's Wednesday evening and shots
have been fired, another intrigue,

another whodunit unfolding
in realtime. The signal

is unbroken. As long as power
flows between the walls

that shelter us, it will be there,
broadcast in digital clarity,

our oracle, our miracle,
the life outside our life.

All we have to do is turn it on
and know we're not involved.

VIII

AS IT IS ON THE EDGE OF TOWN

Just a jump into the long dry grass
of the undeveloped fields

behind the colourless moonscape
of suburban tenements, in that margin

where the city almost ends, people
aren't afraid to leave their trash.

Between the rows of pink and orange
spray-painted property markers

stands a shining white orchard
of cast-off refrigerators, in their day

designed for keeping dead things
dead a little longer, their obsolete

chromium handles and hinges
blindingly bright and burning

to the touch in the heat of noon
as mirages waver in parking lots.

For some it's a place made strange
by the reports of an escaped peacock

that fans its tail and struts and calls out
for its lost mate; for others

it will always be remembered
as the place that boy was found,

finally, and sent home, and laid
to rest in the place he came from.

And still, some see it as it is,
as the land on which the shopping mall

was never built, and where these
poor, pretty children still come

to fly their kites – they come
to witness movement in the heavens,

to witness colour,
and to feel that they control it.

IX

AS IT IS IN THE NOURISHING SOIL

Not far from where the city
stows its dead, winter wheat

breaks through the thaw
to feed the living.

But as more die the graveyard
encroaches on the farm

and one day soon there won't be
room enough for both.

Where to put our mothers
and fathers when the time comes?

Their tombs, because of love,
we imagine assembled

on a plateau of carnations
and marble, and where

carnations will not flower
we must find other ways

to sweeten our grief, or else
to hasten our forgetfulness,

perhaps with work we'll raise
an Everest of crops, and eat

like peasant kings, at least
until our own time comes,

when we are finally lowered
and can begin to repay,

atom by atom,
everything.

X

AS IT IS IN THE EMBRACE OF THE SEA

No one may forget the sunken young,
as the wilderness may not forget

to be full of birdcalls, peaceful places,
decay, and the shaggy

undersides of treetops that scatter
seeds and old leaves

when the branches shiver, as a shark
may not forget to breathe through its gills.

Our memories come on suddenly,
as in the night a television ignites

in the room where we'd fallen asleep
during a power failure – the flickering

wakes us, the voices, the walls awash
with faint and shifting colours,

underwater, unreal, the hallucinations
of our dear ones in the cold embrace

of the sea, where violence itself
is a kind of oxygen, an element

of combustion and sustenance,
while here on the living surface

long months of darkness are coming.
Do not forget: the diving teams

who follow lose their footing
in the waves – and no one

breathing can move so deep
to the slow continuous singing

of the whales.

01 14
J

Notes

"The Armies of Pluto" is dedicated, with apologies, to everyone whose name I've forgotten.

"Brights Grove" (no apostrophe, thank you) is a village on the southern shore of Lake Huron. In the late 1980s, Brights Grove and the surrounding township were assimilated into the Corporation of the City of Sarnia, though most native Grovers still make a distinction.

The title "But I Was Looking at the Permanent Stars" is taken from an unfinished poem found in the manuscripts of Wilfred Owen.

"Girl on a Balcony" was inspired by certain images and poems found in Jennifer LoveGrove's book *The Dagger Between Her Teeth*.

"Girl on a Talk Show (Her Amphibian)" was inspired by episodes of several daytime talk shows dealing with the subject of unwanted pregnancy.

"Take 1 Tablet(s) Daily": Paroxetine HCl (hydrochloride) is the antidepressant sold under the trade name Paxil.

"Tall Man with Dog and Rabbits": This poem is for Chris Banks.

Acknowledgements

I gratefully acknowledge the citizens of Canada through the Canada Council for the Arts and the citizens of Ontario through the Ontario Arts Council for financial assistance during the writing of this book.

Some of these poems, often in different versions or with different titles, first appeared in the following publications: *Dandelion*, *Dig*, *Echolocation*, *Existere*, *The Fiddlehead*, *Ink Magazine*, *The Instant Anthology*, *Kiss Machine*, *The Literary Review of Canada*, *Matrix*, *The Mike*, *Modomnoc*, *Nthposition*, *Other Poetry* (U.K.), *Queen Street Quarterly*, *Taddle Creek*, the poetry anthology *In the Criminal's Cabinet* (nthposition, 2004), and the chapbook *Widows & Orphans* (Junction Books, 2002). My thanks to the editors of each.

Many thanks to the following people, all of whom were helpful during the writing of the poems in this book: Chris Banks, Evie Christie, Peter Darbyshire, Michael Holmes, Dennis Lee, A.J. Levin, Ronan Quinn, Martha Sharpe, John Stiles, Anne F. Walker, Silas White, Carleton Wilson, Patrick Woodcock, and Mary-lou Zeitoun.

Special thanks to A.F. Moritz for his editorial suggestions, and also to Ellen Seligman and Anita Chong at McClelland & Stewart.

As always, I am most grateful to my family, Percy, Carol, Shelley, and Jodi, whose love and support I could not do without.